THE JESUS BOOK

Published in Nashville, Tennessee, by Thomas Nelson. Thomas Nelson is a registered trademark of Thomas Nelson, Inc.

Illustrated by Claudine Gevry.

Thomas Nelson, Inc., titles may be purchased in bulk for educational, business, fund-raising, or sales promotional use. For information, please e-mail SpecialMarkets@ThomasNelson.com.

Library of Congress Cataloging-in-Publication Data

Elkins, Stephen.
  The Jesus book / by Stephen Elkins ; illustrated by Claudine Gévry.
    p. cm.
  Includes bibliographical references and index.
  ISBN 978-1-4003-1463-8 (hardcover with cd)
  1. Jesus Christ—Juvenile literature. I. Gévry, Claudine. II. Title.
  BT302.E39 2009
  232—dc22   2009018133

Printed in the United States of America

09 10 11 12 LBM 6 5 4 3 2 1

THE JESUS BOOK

By Stephen Elkins

Illustrated by Claudine Gevry

THOMAS NELSON®
Since 1798

NASHVILLE DALLAS MEXICO CITY RIO DE JANEIRO BEIJING

CONTENTS

CONTENTS

JESUS

For God loved the world so much that
he gave his only Son. God gave his
Son so that whoever believes in him may
not be lost, but have eternal life.

—John 3:16

Dear Parents,

The Jesus Book was written to help teach children about the life of Christ and how to enter a life-long relationship with him. For the purpose of this book, the stories were written in past tense as they refer to specific events that happened when Jesus was walking on the earth. However, we are blessed to serve a risen Savior who holds the same power today to heal, bless, and forgive as he did 2,000 years ago.

I hope you and your children enjoy this book and are blessed by his presence.

Sincerely,
Stephen Elkins

WHO JESUS IS

The prophets said Jesus was
The Promised One.

Isaiah 9:6

The prophets were messengers for God. They told about things that would happen in the future. Isaiah was one of the greatest prophets. He lived 800 years before Jesus was born. But listen to the words Isaiah wrote about Jesus: "A child will be born to us. God will give a son to us. . . . His name will be Wonderful Counselor, Powerful God, Father Who Loves Forever, Prince of Peace."

Through Isaiah, God gave us the wonderful promise of Jesus. But Isaiah wasn't the only prophet who spoke about Jesus. Micah told where he would be born; Zechariah said his side would be pierced; David said he would be crucified.

And they all said that some day the **Promised One** would come!

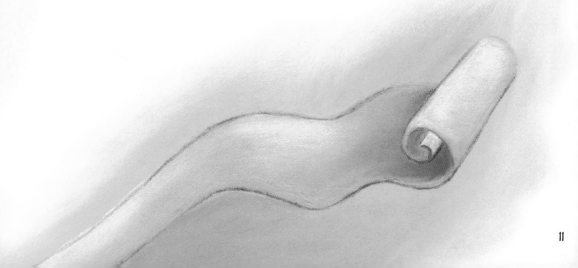

The angel said Jesus was
The Son of God.

Luke 1:26–38

More than 300 prophecies had been written about the Messiah who would come. Jesus was coming soon! And God's very special plan would include a young Jewish girl named Mary. God sent the angel Gabriel to visit Mary.

Seeing an angel might frighten anyone! So Gabriel said, "Don't be afraid, Mary, because God is pleased with you. Listen! . . . You will give birth to a son, and you will name him Jesus. . . . He will be called the **Son of God**." Mary trusted God and she said, "Let this happen to me as you say!" Then the angel went away as quickly as he had appeared.

The wise men said Jesus was
The King of the Jews.

Matthew 2:1–12

After the birth of Jesus, **magi**, or wise men from the east, made their way to Jerusalem to find the King of kings. God sent a bright star to lead them to Jesus. When they arrived in Jerusalem, they asked, "Where is the baby who was born to be the **king of the Jews**? . . . We came to worship him."

Upon seeing Jesus, they knelt down and worshiped him. And they offered him these gifts: gold, which was a fitting gift for a king; frankincense, which was a healing medicine; and myrrh, which was a perfume used in burials.

Such perfect gifts for the king who would heal his people and then one day die on a cross to save them.

Peter said Jesus was
The Christ.

Mark 8:27–29

Who is Jesus? The people who saw Jesus do miracles on earth asked this question, and people today still ask it. One day, Jesus asked his disciples, "Who do people say I am?"

They answered, "Some people say you are John the Baptist. Others say you are Elijah. And others say that you are one of the prophets."

But Jesus was much more than a man. He had come from heaven. So Jesus asked, "Who do you say I am?"

Peter answered, "You are **the Christ.**" Peter believed that Jesus was more than a man. He was the promised Messiah, the Son of the living God, sent from heaven.

Peter understood who Jesus was and where Jesus had come from!

John the Baptist said Jesus was
The Lamb of God.

John 1:28–31; Matthew 3:1–6

He wore clothes made of camel hair. He ate locusts and wild honey and lived in the desert. He was John the Baptist. And it was John's job to prepare the people for the coming of Jesus.

One day, as John stood baptizing sinners in the Jordan River, he saw Jesus walking down the hillside toward him. John said, "Look, the Lamb of God. He takes away the sins of the world!" John called Jesus the Lamb of God because—like the lambs that were sacrificed in the Old Testament times—Jesus would be offered as a sacrifice to save his people.

The Samaritans said Jesus was
The Savior of the world.

John 4:1–42

In the days of Jesus, Jews and Samaritans lived in the same region but were divided from each other. They did not associate with one another. A Jewish person would not even talk to a Samaritan . . . but Jesus did.

One day Jesus, a Jew, met a Samaritan woman at a well. Jesus said to her, "Please give me a drink."

The woman was surprised because Jesus spoke to her with kindness. As they began to talk, Jesus told the Samaritan woman many things about herself. The woman said, "I know that the Messiah is coming."

Then Jesus said, "He is talking to you now. I am he."

The Samaritan woman believed. She brought her friends to Jesus, and they believed too, saying, "This man really is **the Savior of the world.**"

God the Father said Jesus was
His beloved Son.

Mark 1:9–11

Don't you just love it when your father is pleased with you? There's joy that comes with hearing the words "I'm proud of you!" Did you know that Jesus' Father was pleased with him? When Jesus came to John the Baptist to be baptized, John was confused. He knew that Jesus always did what was right and had no need of baptism.

But Jesus assured John that it was the right thing to do. And as Jesus came up out of the water, a voice spoke from heaven. It was his Father's voice. And he said, "You are **my Son** and I love you. I am very pleased with you."

God is always pleased when we do his will.

John the disciple said Jesus was
The Word.

John 1:1; 14:9; Luke 13:3

The very first verse in the book of John tells us who Jesus is. John calls him "**the Word.**" Words help us understand things. Words describe things others have not seen, and words can save us from dangerous situations. For example, we shout, "Stop!" to prevent an accident.

John calls Jesus "the Word" because it is Jesus who helps us understand who God is. We haven't seen God, but Jesus tells us about God when he says, "He who has seen me has seen the Father." It is Jesus who tells us about heaven, and it is Jesus who saves us from the dangers of sin. "Change your hearts and lives!" he warns.

Jesus is the walking, talking, living, breathing Word of God.

WHO JESUS IS

Jesus said he is
Our friend.

John 15:12–15

Friends love to be together. They play together, spend time on the phone talking together, and help each other at school. Even when bad days come, friends stick together. The Bible says to have a friend you must show yourself to be a friend. If we are going to show our friendship, we must do something for others.

Jesus said, "I call you **friends**." And to show himself as a friend, he did an amazing thing. He said, "The greatest love a person can show is to die for his friends." Jesus not only called us his friends, he showed us. He showed that he was our friend by dying on a cross to save us from our sins.

Wow! What a friend we have in Jesus!

Jesus said he is . . .

The bread that gives life. —John 6:35
The light of the world. —John 8:12
The Good Shepherd. —John 10:11–15
The way, truth, and life. —John 14:6
The vine. —John 15:5

Jesus described himself in many ways so people would know who he is. He said, "I am **the bread that gives life**," because in the same way bread fills an empty stomach, Jesus fills an empty heart. Jesus called himself "**the light of the world**," because those who follow him will never live in darkness.

He is **the Good Shepherd** because he takes care of us, and he is **the Way** because he guides us. He said, "I am **the vine**, and you are the branches," because when we stay connected to Jesus, he provides the strength we need.

Jesus has many names, but only one purpose: he came to save us by being our bread, light, shepherd, vine, and way.

Jesus is everything we need.

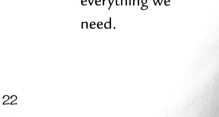

WHAT JESUS DID

He healed many.

Matthew 8:1–3

Have you ever scraped your knee? It hurts! And it takes days to heal naturally. But when Jesus healed people, something supernatural happened. He healed them quickly and completely. The blind could see—immediately! Those who could not walk got up and walked—immediately! Natural healing can be slow, but the supernatural healing of Jesus was quick and complete.

One day a man with a skin disease came and knelt before Jesus. He said, "Lord, you have the power to heal me if you want." He knew Jesus was able to heal him, but he asked Jesus if he were willing.

Jesus touched the man and said, "I want to heal you. **Be healed!**" Immediately the man was healed!

The power to heal belongs to Jesus.

He raised the dead.

Luke 8:41–56

Jairus was worried because his daughter was sick. So he went to the One he knew could heal her. But before Jesus could get to Jairus's house, something terrible happened. Some men came to tell Jairus that his daughter had died. But Jesus paid no attention to what the men said. Instead, he spoke words that gave Jairus hope: "Don't be afraid. Just believe."

Taking Peter, James, and John with him, Jesus continued on to the home of Jairus. Together they went into the room where the lifeless body of the little girl lay. Then Jesus took her hand and said, "My child, stand up!" Immediately she stood up!

Even the **power of life** and death belongs to Jesus.

He ruled over nature.

He Calmed the Storm; Luke 8:22–25

Storms can be very frightening, can't they? There was a terrible storm that even frightened Jesus' disciples. They were out on the lake in a boat. Waves crashed and the wind roared. And where was Jesus? He was in the back of the boat, fast asleep. The disciples woke him, saying, "Master! Master! We will drown!" Jesus got up and **commanded** the wind and waves to be still. And in an instant, all was calm.

The One who created the winds and waves can certainly control them.

On another day the disciples set out across the lake in a boat. It was dark when a powerful wind began to toss the boat on the water. They rowed harder and harder, but it was no use. They could not get the boat to shore. Then they saw Jesus. He was walking toward them on the water! He said, **"It is I! Do not be afraid."** Then Jesus got into the boat, and the wind became calm.

The One who made the waves can certainly walk on them.

He fed 5,000.

Mark 6:30–44; John 6:1–13

The news of Jesus' miracles began to spread. People came from everywhere to hear him teach. One day Jesus taught until late in the day. His disciples told Jesus to send the people away so they could get food. But to their surprise, Jesus said, "You give them food to eat."

The disciples didn't know how they were going to feed so many people. All they had was a boy's lunch of five loaves and two fish. But Jesus took the food, blessed it, and began breaking it into pieces. More than **5,000** people were fed that day with twelve baskets of food left over.

Jesus fed everyone with a small boy's lunch!

He forgave sin.

Mark 2:1–12

Jesus had the power to heal. He could make blind eyes see and deaf ears hear. But Jesus had the power to heal men's souls as well as their bodies. We call sickness of the soul **sin**. And Jesus proved to a crowd that he had the cure for sin.

One day some men carried their friend to see Jesus, because the man was lame and they hoped Jesus would heal him. But when they got to the house where Jesus was, the crowd was too big. They could not get inside. So they climbed onto the roof, cut out a large hole, and lowered their friend down on a mat. Jesus saw the man's crippled legs, but he knew this man needed more than healing for his body—he needed healing for his soul! Jesus said, "Your sins are forgiven."

The Pharisees were angry. They said to themselves, "Only God can forgive sins." Jesus knew what they were thinking and said, "I will prove to you that the Son of Man has authority on earth to forgive sins." He commanded the lame man to stand up. The man stood and walked away with his mat!

Jesus has the power to forgive sin because he is the Son of God.

He went to the cross.

Hebrews 9:22

Death is not something we like to think about much. But it is important to remember this: though salvation was freely given, it did not come to us without a great cost. And that cost is talked about in Hebrews 9:22: "And sins cannot be forgiven without blood to show death."

It isn't a pleasant thing to think about, but our **salvation** cost Jesus his life. Jesus died on a cross for me and for you. He did it so our sins could be forgiven, and so that one day we could live with him in heaven forever! Jesus obeyed his Father and went to the cross, shedding his blood for you and me.

What a price Jesus paid for us!

He rose from the dead.

Matthew 28:1–8

Jesus died on a dark Friday evening. Those who loved him watched as his body was taken down from the cross. Many of his followers thought all was lost and that maybe they had made a mistake. Maybe Jesus wasn't the Messiah. But they didn't know that Sunday morning was coming.

Mary Magdalene and another woman named Mary were the first to visit Jesus' tomb that Sunday. The large stone covering the entrance had been rolled away, and an angel spoke to them: "I know that you are looking for Jesus, the one who was killed on the cross. But he is not here. **He has risen.**" The women ran to tell the disciples.

And that's what we must do. We must tell the world Jesus has risen from the dead.

He brought salvation to the world.

Acts 4:12

What does the word *salvation* mean? It means you have been rescued. Rescued from what? Let's pretend that you have become very sick. The doctor says only one medicine can save you. Would you take it? Of course you would!

Jesus is like a good medicine. We all have a condition called *sin*. Sin leads to death and separation from God. The Bible teaches us that "Jesus is the only One who can save people. . . . And we must be saved through him!" That means **only Jesus can save us** from sin. He saves us like a good medicine.

When we invite him into our hearts, Jesus becomes our salvation.

He is preparing a home for me.

John 13:36–14:2; Revelations 1:14

There were times when Jesus' disciples didn't understand some of the things Jesus said. When Jesus said he was going away, they were troubled. "Where are you going?" Peter asked.

Jesus answered, "Don't let your hearts be troubled. Trust in God." Then Jesus began to speak about a place called heaven. "There are many rooms in my Father's house," he said. "I am going there to prepare a place for you."

And do you know what? Jesus is preparing a place in **heaven** for you too! Just think, your home in heaven may be next door to Peter's house!

Jesus is busy getting everything ready so that when we move out of this world, we can move right into his!

WHAT JESUS TAUGHT

He taught using parables.

Matthew 7:24–27; 13:13, 31–32;
Luke 10:30–37; 15:1–10

All great teachers have one thing in common. They make their lessons easy to understand. That is why Jesus was the greatest teacher of all. He used simple parables to teach many of his greatest lessons.

Parables are short stories that use common, everyday things to teach about God's kingdom. Jesus used a mustard seed to teach about faith. Stories of lost sheep and coins were used to teach about God's forgiveness. He told stories about good neighbors and vineyards and building houses to teach us how to live godly lives.

Yes, Jesus used ordinary things to teach extraordinary lessons.

He taught about baptism.

Matthew 3

When Jesus was a little boy, the Greeks had a word they used on laundry days. The word was *bapto*. *Bapto* was the word used when a piece of clothing was dipped in bleach and then into a dye. The bleach cleaned the cloth, and then the dye gave it a new color.

The word *baptism* comes from the Greek word *bapto*. Baptism is an outward sign that we have been **cleaned** and **changed** on the inside. We have been cleansed from sin and changed because we have asked Jesus into our hearts.

Because of Jesus, all our sins have been washed away.

He taught about repentance.

Matthew 4:17

Jesus tells us to *repent*, which means we choose to change ourselves for God. Jesus said, "Change your hearts and lives, because the kingdom of heaven is coming soon."

When we repent, we do two very important things: First, we change our hearts. That changes how we think. We come to see that our way of doing things is not like God's way. So then we change what we do. Instead of doing the things that please us, we choose to do the things that please God. To repent means we **change our hearts**, and we change our lives. We turn away from sin and turn toward God.

Repent! Now that's a real change.

He taught us to pray.

Matthew 6:5–13

One day my best friend came to me with some frightening news. The school principal wanted to talk to me. As I entered his office and stood in front of his big desk, I was scared. But he smiled and said, "Congratulations, Stephen! You are student of the month." Whew! This very important and powerful man just wanted to talk to me.

God is like that. He is very important and powerful, and he wants to talk to you! How? Through prayer.

Jesus teaches us how to pray. First, we should **praise** God.

"Our Father in heaven, we pray that your name will always be kept holy."

Then we should **ask** God to help us do what he wants us to do.

"We pray that your kingdom will come. We pray that what you want will be done, here on earth as it is in heaven."

Jesus said we should then ask God for the things we need.

"Give us the food we need for each day."

We should also **confess** our sins.

"Forgive the sins we have done, just as we have forgiven those who did wrong to us."

Finally, we should ask God to lead us every day and to keep us safe from the Evil One.

"Do not cause us to be tested; but save us from the Evil One."

Remember, God loves you, and he wants you to talk to him every day!

He taught the Golden Rule.

Matthew 7:12

Which would you want? A truckload of pennies or a couple of gold bricks? Gold bricks? Good choice! Gold is very valuable, and that's why "the Golden Rule" is called golden! It teaches us a lesson of **great value**: "Do for other people the same things you want them to do for you."

Jesus was saying we should treat others as we would like to be treated. Would you like someone to cut in front of you in line or take the toys you are using? No! Treat others the way you want to be treated! It's easy to say, but a little harder to do. But once you get the hang of it, the Golden Rule can make you rich in love!

Treating others well pleases Jesus!

He taught the Greatest Commandment.

Matthew 22:36–39

Jesus was once asked which commandment was the greatest. He answered, "'**Love the Lord** your God with all your heart, soul and mind.' This is the first and most important command. And the second command is like the first: '**Love your neighbor** as you love yourself.'"

Jesus knew that love was the answer. People who love each other don't steal from each other. People who love each other don't lie to each other. If we love God, we will show our love by serving and obeying him. And if we love each other, we will show our love by doing what is right.

Ask God to teach you to love!

He taught us to go and tell the Good News.

Matthew 28:16–20

Come and see! We hear that a lot today. But Jesus taught his believers to do just the opposite. Just before he left to go back to heaven, Jesus told his disciples to go and tell! He said, "Go and make followers of all people in the world." This is the great common mission, or the **Great Commission**, we have as Christians.

We must go and tell! The goal of every Christian is not to get people to come and see. Our goal is to get people into God's kingdom by going and telling them about God's love. We may go next door, or to another city, or even to another country. And Jesus promised that as we go, he will always be with us.

Jesus wants us to go and tell others about him.

He taught that he loves us.

John 13:34

We've all sung the words "Jesus loves me, this I know." But do we know how much? To Jesus, *love* is an **action** word. He said, "You must love each other as I have loved you."

Jesus showed his love for us when he left his heavenly home and came to earth as a man. He suffered because he loved us. He was made fun of because he loved us. He preached the truth while people told lies about him, all because he loved us. And eventually, he went to a cross to die. And why did Jesus do all of this? It's an easy four-letter word: **love**!

"Jesus loves me, this I know, for the Bible tells me so."

He taught that he will never leave me.

Matthew 28:20; John 3:8

Jesus has made this promise to you: "You can be sure that I will be with you always." What a comforting promise! But sometimes we forget he's here because we can't see him! I've learned a way that helps me know **Jesus is always with me**. I think of the wind. You can't see the wind, but you know it's there when you see the leaves rustling in the breeze.

Jesus is like the wind. You can't see him, but you can see all the wonderful things he has made, and you can see him at work in the lives of his children. And one day you will see Jesus in person—coming in the clouds to take his children home for all eternity!

WHEN IT HAPPENED

In the beginning God created
the sky and the earth.

—Genesis 1:1

600–500 BC

Zechariah the prophet said that Jesus' side
would be pierced or stabbed: "They will look at
me, the one they have stabbed. . . . They will be as
sad as someone who has lost a firstborn son."

—Zechariah 12:10

0–5 AD

The angel Gabriel told Mary she would have
a son, and he would be the Son of God. "You
will give birth to a son, and you will name
him Jesus. He will be great, and people will
call him the Son of the Most High."

—Luke 1:31b–32a

The Baby Jesus was born! "While Joseph
and Mary were in Bethlehem, the time
came for her to have the baby. She
gave birth to her first son."

—Luke 2:6–7a.

The angels visited the shepherds, and
the shepherds went to see Baby Jesus in the
manger. "So the shepherds went quickly and
found Mary and Joseph."

—Luke 2:16

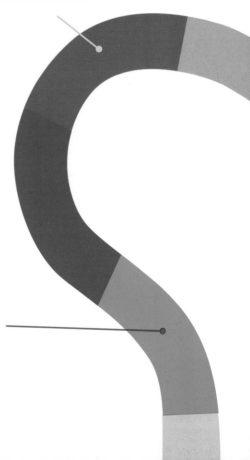

1500–1400 BC
Moses said this about Jesus:
"The Lord your God will give you a prophet like me.
He will be one of your own people. Listen to him."
—Deuteronomy 18:15

800–700 BC
Micah said Jesus would be born
in Bethlehem: "But you, Bethlehem
Ephrathah, are one of the
smallest towns in Judah. But from
you will come one who will rule
Israel for me. . . ."
—Micah 5:2

800–700 BC
Isaiah said, "A child will be born to us. God
will give a son to us. . . . His name will be
Wonderful Counselor, Powerful God, Father
Who lives Forever, Prince of Peace."
—Isaiah 9:6

WHEN IT HAPPENED

13–17 AD

Jesus and his family went to Jerusalem for the Passover Feast. "When Jesus was 12 years old, they went to the feast as they always did."

—Luke 2:42

30–35 AD

Jesus was baptized by John the Baptist. "When all the people were being baptized by John, Jesus also was baptized."

—Luke 3:21a

"When Jesus began to teach, he was about 30 years old."

—Luke 3:23a

And now . . .

Jesus is preparing a home for us. "There are many rooms in my Father's house. I would not tell you this if it were not true. I am going there to prepare a place for you."

Someday, Jesus promised to come back for us! "After I go and prepare a place for you, I will come back. Then I will take you to be with me so that you may be where I am."

—John 14:2–3

"Jesus went everywhere in Galilee. He taught in the synagogues and preached the Good News about the kingdom of heaven. And he healed all the people's diseases and sicknesses."

—Matthew 4:23

The Pharisees planned to kill Jesus.
"Then the leading priests and Pharisees called a meeting of the Jewish council. They asked, 'What should we do? This man is doing many miracles. If we let him continue doing these things, everyone will believe in him. Then the Romans will come and take away our temple and our nation'. . . . That day they started planning to kill Jesus."

—John 11:47–48, 53

Jesus was crucified on the cross. "Jesus cried out in a loud voice, 'Father, I give you my life.' After Jesus said this, he died."

—Luke 23:46

Jesus rose again! The angel said, "Jesus is not here. He has risen from death!"

—Luke 24:6a

Jesus gave us the Great Commission: "So go and make followers of all people in the world. Baptize them in the name of the Father and the Son and the Holy Spirit."

—Matthew 28:19

When did Moses speak about Jesus?

Deuteronomy 18:15; John 1:45; 5:45–46; Luke 24:27

Jesus said he was the Son of God. The Jews wanted proof. According to the Law of Moses, Jesus needed a witness to speak on his behalf. So Jesus told the Jews that Moses had written about him. Fourteen hundred years before Jesus was born, Moses wrote, "The Lord your God will give you a prophet like me. He will be one of your own people. Listen to him."

How was Jesus like Moses? They were both prophets, priests, lawgivers, and leaders of men. They both taught new truths and new commandments. And they both performed miracles. After Philip met Jesus, he found Nathanael and told him, "Remember that **Moses wrote in the law** about a man who was coming. . . . We have found him. He is Jesus."

When was Jesus born?

Galatians 4:4

God's timing is always perfect. He is never too early or too late. He is never in a hurry and—unlike you and me—he is always on time. The Bible says that "when the right time came, God sent his Son." Through the ages, God had been preparing the world for the **coming of Jesus**.

Many prophets had told about Jesus' coming, and the Jewish people were watching for the promised Messiah. The world was united under Roman rule, and the Romans had built good roads to every part of the world. Greek was a common language. All of this was just perfect for spreading Jesus' message of hope to people everywhere!

Jesus was indeed born at just the right time!

When did Jesus' ministry begin?

Matthew 3:13–17; Acts 2

The word *ministry* means "to serve." Jesus' ministry began at the Jordan River right after he was baptized. As he came up out of the water, heaven opened and **God's Spirit** came down on him like a dove. At that moment, his earthly ministry began.

And the same thing happened to the disciples and to the first Christian church after Jesus went back to heaven. God's Spirit came down on a day called Pentecost, when 3,000 people were saved!

Jesus' ministry began when God's Spirit came to him, and ours does too.

When did Nicodemus come to Jesus?

John 3:1–21

Nicodemus was a wise ruler of the Jewish temple. He wanted to know more about Jesus, so he arranged to meet Jesus **at night**. "We know that you are a teacher sent from God," Nicodemus said.

Jesus answered him in a curious way: "I tell you the truth. Unless one is born again, he cannot be in God's kingdom."

Puzzled, Nicodemus asked, "But if a man is already old, how can he be born again?"

Now when a baby is born, he leaves the darkness of his mother's womb and comes out into the light. Jesus was telling Nicodemus that to be in God's kingdom you must come out of this dark world and be born into the light of God's kingdom.

When did Peter deny Jesus?

Luke 22:31-62

Peter thought his faith was strong. He said, "Lord, I am ready to go to prison with you. I will even die for you." But Jesus said to him, "Before the rooster crows tonight, you will say you don't know me. You will say this three times!"

Peter couldn't believe it. That very night Jesus was arrested. It was very frightening. The disciples knew prisoners were sometimes beaten and even killed.

So when a young girl recognized **Peter** as one of Jesus' followers, Peter said, "Girl, I don't know him." Three times Peter said he didn't know Jesus. The third time, while Peter was still speaking, a rooster crowed.

Then Peter remembered what Jesus had said, and he was filled with shame.

When was Jesus raised from the dead?

Luke 23:46; Matthew 12:40; Luke 24

Many heard Jesus speak his last words, "Father, I give you my life." After he said this, Jesus died. Some remembered Jesus saying, "Jonah was in the stomach of the big fish for three days and three nights. In the same way, the Son of Man will be in the grave three days and three nights." Jesus had said that he would rise from the dead. Would it actually happen?

On that Sunday, **three days after Jesus died**, Mary Magdalene and some other women found the tomb of Jesus empty. Where was he? An angel appeared to Mary Magdalene and told her he had risen! But did anyone see him alive? Yes!

The Bible tells us that Jesus appeared to many people!

When did Thomas believe Jesus was risen?

John 20:24–29

The other disciples had already seen the risen Jesus, but Thomas had not. They told Thomas that Jesus was alive! But he told them, "I will not believe it until I see the nail marks in his hands."

A week later Jesus suddenly appeared to the disciples. He looked at Thomas and said, "Put your finger here. Look at my hands. Put your hand here in my side. Stop doubting and believe." Thomas was now sure it was true . . . Jesus was alive!

Jesus said to Thomas, "You believe because you see me. Those who believe without seeing me will be truly happy."

WHERE IT HAPPENED

The Israel Region

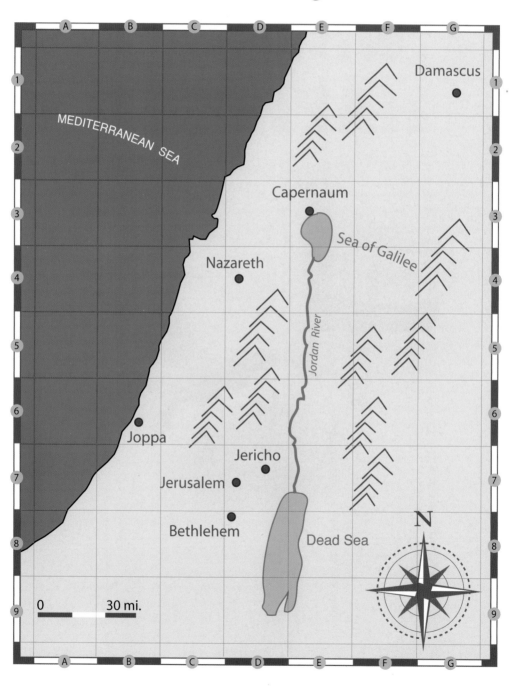

Can you find?

Where did Jesus grow up?

Nazareth	D·4
Jerusalem	D·7
The Sea of Galilee	E·3
The Jordan River	E·3–7
Bethlehem	D·8
Damascus	G·1
Capernaum	E·3
Joppa	B·6
Jericho	D·7
The Dead Sea	D–E·7–9

Where was Jesus born?

By what body of water did Jesus call his disciiples?

Jerusalem (about 30 AD)

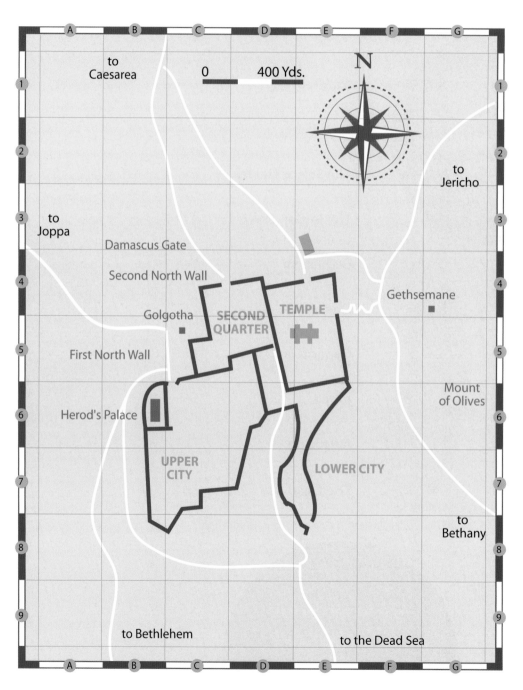

to Caesarea

0   400 Yds.

N

to Jericho

to Joppa

Damascus Gate

Second North Wall

Golgotha

SECOND QUARTER

TEMPLE

Gethsemane

First North Wall

Mount of Olives

Herod's Palace

UPPER CITY

LOWER CITY

to Bethany

to Bethlehem

to the Dead Sea

Can you find?

Gethsemane	G·4
Golgotha	C·5
The Temple	E·5
Herod's Palace	B·6
The Mount of Olives	G·6

Where did Jesus go to pray?

Do you know where Jesus died on the cross?

Can you find where Jesus taught as a boy?

Where was Jesus born?

Luke 2:1–7; Micah 5:2–5

Augustus Caesar wanted to know how many people lived in his kingdom. So he commanded everyone to return to their hometown to be counted. Joseph and Mary were among those making the journey from Nazareth to the town of Bethlehem.

Bethlehem was called the City of David. And since Joseph was related to King David, Bethlehem was considered his hometown. They traveled through several villages and five miles past Jerusalem to the little town of Bethlehem where Jesus was born.

Many years before, the prophet Micah had said that a ruler would come out of Bethlehem who would take care of his people. Jesus was that great ruler!

Where did Jesus grow up?

Mark 1:9; Luke 1:26–27; John 1:45–46

Nazareth was a small town in the north of Israel, settled in a valley with hills all around it. It was there that the angel Gabriel visited Mary to tell her that she would be the mother of Jesus. He was known to many as Jesus the Nazarene because **Nazareth** was his childhood home. When Philip told Nathanael that Jesus was from Nazareth, he remarked, "Nazareth! Can anything good come from Nazareth?"

But we know that something good did come from Nazareth: salvation through our Lord Jesus Christ. In fact, it's better than good!

Salvation is the greatest gift of all!

Where did Jesus teach as a boy?

Luke 2:41–52

When Jesus was twelve years old, Mary and Joseph took him to **Jerusalem** to celebrate the Passover. They stayed for several days. In those days, it was common for large groups of families to travel together. So as Mary and Joseph headed home, they thought Jesus was with their group. When they couldn't find him, they hurried back to Jerusalem. After three days they found him **in the temple**, where the teachers were amazed at his knowledge.

When Mary told Jesus they had been worried, Jesus answered, "You should have known that I must be where my Father's work is!" Jesus returned to Nazareth where he continued to learn more and to grow. As he grew up people liked him, and God was pleased with him.

Where was Jesus baptized?

Matthew 3:13–17

It starts where two rivers from Lebanon and Syria meet. Its waters flow 156 miles through the valleys and plains of Israel into the Sea of Galilee. On it goes to the south where it ends at the Dead Sea. It's called the **Jordan River**. It is the largest and longest river in Israel and the only river in Israel that is never dry.

The Bible says Jesus came to the Jordan River to be baptized by John. John said, "I should be baptized by you!"

But Jesus answered, "Let it be this way for now. We should do all things that are right."

So there in the Jordan River, close to where its waters enter the Sea of Galilee, Jesus was baptized.

Where was Jesus tempted by the devil?

Matthew 4:1–11

God the Father was pleased as Jesus' ministry began. But the devil was not! Jesus went into the **wilderness** to fast and pray; the devil waited for his chance to tempt him. The wilderness of Judea was an area close to the Dead Sea. It is very dry and rocky.

After Jesus had fasted for forty days, the devil appeared to him. He tempted our Lord in every way possible. But Jesus answered each temptation by quoting the Word of God. "Go away from me, Satan!" said Jesus. "It is written in the Scriptures, 'You must worship the Lord your God. Serve only him!'"

That's how you defeat the devil. When the devil is heard—just speak the Word of God!

Where did Jesus call many of his disciples?

Mark 1:16–20; Luke 5:27–28; Acts 1:11

There is a body of water in Israel called the **Sea of Galilee**. It is a place Jesus knew well. He walked on its stormy waters. He spoke to the waves, and they were quieted. Once, he met several fishermen on its shores. "Come and follow me," Jesus said. Peter and Andrew followed. Later he called James and John, and they followed him too. Jesus had twelve disciples.

Where did the other disciples who followed Jesus come from? Six more also came from the area of Galilee: Philip and his friend Nathanael; Thomas, known as doubting Thomas; James, the son of Alpheus; Judas, son of James; and Simon the Zealot. Matthew, the tax collector, came from Capernaum. Judas Iscariot, the one who betrayed Jesus, came from Judea.

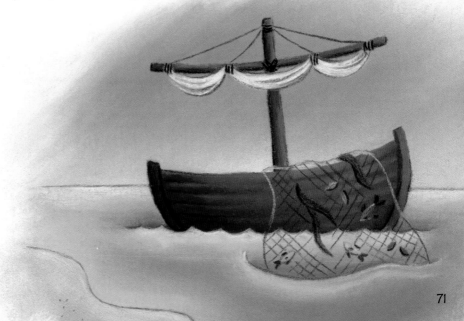

Where did Jesus bless the children?

Matthew 19:13–14

Although Jesus was born in Bethlehem in Judea, he grew up in Nazareth, a small village in Galilee. Just think of Judea and Galilee as states, and Bethlehem and Nazareth as cities within those states. It was in **Judea** that Jesus blessed the children.

The people of Judea brought their children to Jesus. They wanted Jesus to pray for them. But his disciples thought Jesus was too busy, and they tried to send the children away. When Jesus saw this, he said, "Let the little children come to me. Don't stop them, because the kingdom of heaven belongs to people who are like these children."

And what are children like, you ask? They are people who trust in their heavenly Father.

Where did Jesus go to pray?

Matthew 26:36–50

There was a garden of olive trees at the base of the Mount of Olives, outside the walls of Jerusalem. It was called the **Garden of Gethsemane.** This was the place where Jesus went to pray the night he was arrested.

Peter, James, and John went with Jesus into the garden that night. Jesus asked them to watch and pray, but they fell asleep. Jesus prayed, "My Father, if it is not possible for this painful thing to be taken from me, and if I must do it, then I pray that what you want will be done."

Soon after this prayer, the soldiers came for Jesus. They followed Judas, who had led them to where Jesus was.

Where did Jesus die on a cross?

Mark 15:22; John 19:17–30

The place where Jesus died has a name that sends shivers up my spine; it is **Golgotha**, which means the "Place of the Skull"! It was a horrible place outside the walls of the city of Jerusalem. There, criminals who had done terrible things were punished. What in the world was Jesus doing in a place like that? He was showing his love for us.

On the hill called Golgotha, Jesus was crucified between two thieves. His mother, Mary, and his beloved disciple John listened as Jesus spoke his last words: "It is finished." After saying this, Jesus died.

Golgotha: It still sends shivers up my spine. Just think, the Son of God shed his blood for you and me!

Where is Jesus now?

Acts 1:1–11; John 14:1–2

After three days in the tomb, Jesus rose from the dead. He then spent forty days on earth encouraging his disciples and friends. He told his disciples that they were to tell the whole world what he had taught them. And after Jesus said this, his disciples watched as he rose up into the sky.

They were still looking up when two men in white robes appeared and said to them, "Why are you standing here looking into the sky? You saw Jesus taken away from you into heaven. He will come back in the same way you saw him go."

For Jesus had said, "There are many rooms in my Father's house. . . . I am going there to prepare a place for you."

Where can we find God's kingdom?

Matthew 6:10; Luke 17:21

Jesus prayed to God his Father, "We pray that your kingdom will come." What did he mean?

A kingdom is a place where a king rules. And a kingdom must have people who are willing to obey and serve the king. God's kingdom is the place where God rules. So we find God's kingdom wherever we find people who honor him as ruler of their lives.

Jesus said, "God's kingdom is coming, but not in a way that you will be able to see with your eyes." That's because God's kingdom is within us.

We find God's kingdom in the **hearts** of those who honor him as king.

WHY IT HAPPENED

Why did Mary name her baby Jesus?

Luke 1:30–31; Matthew 1:20–21

When God makes a plan, no detail is left out. So when he planned to send a Savior into this world, he had just the right name picked out. What was it?

When the angel Gabriel first appeared to Mary, he told her, "You will give birth to a son, and you will name him Jesus." Later an angel also appeared to Joseph in a dream. The angel said, "Joseph . . . [Mary] will give birth to a son. You will name the son Jesus. Give him that name because he will save his people from their sins."

The name *Jesus* is Greek for the Hebrew name *Yeshua,* which means: "God saves." What the angel said to Joseph was this: Call his name "God saves" because he will save his people from their sins.

So Mary and Joseph **obeyed** the command of God. They named this child—who had been sent from God—Jesus.

Mary named her baby Jesus in obedience to God.

Why was Jesus sent?

Luke 19:10

When something exciting happens in your life, something really great, what do you want to do? Do you clam up and zip your lips? Or do you rush to tell all your friends? Of course you want to tell everyone! And that's exactly what Jesus did. Jesus was sent from heaven with some really good news! And for three years, he preached that good news to anyone who would listen.

Jesus said he came "to find lost people and save them." To be "lost" means that you have not heard about God's love. To be "saved" means that you have heard and received God's love by inviting Jesus into your heart. It means you will live with Jesus forever in heaven. That's the Good News—the best news! So now that you know why Jesus came, let's go tell everyone!

Jesus came to make God known to us.

Why did Jesus love children?

Matthew 18:1–4; Matthew 6:25

Little children are very special to Jesus. He once told his followers, "You must change and become like little children. If you don't do this, you will never enter the kingdom of heaven."

So what did Jesus see in little children that he did not see in adults? **Little children have great faith.** They look to their parents to provide all that they need. Without worry, they depend on them for food, clothes, and a place to live. Their faith in their parents is strong and never wavers.

Like children, everyone should depend on their heavenly Father for those very same things. "Don't worry," Jesus said. Depend on the Father for what you need. Children can do it. Can you?

Yes, there are some things that kids do much better than adults. And having faith is one of them.

Jesus loves children and wants everyone to have their great faith.

Why does Jesus have authority on earth?

Mark 11:15–17; John 3:35; 5:27; 11:43–44

When an army officer shouts an order to his men, they obey! They do this because of a nine-letter word called *authority*. When you have authority, you have the power to tell others what to do.

Jesus had great authority. He had authority over sickness. When he said, "Be healed," the sickness had to leave. Jesus had authority over life and death. When he saw money changers buying and selling in the church, he stopped it. Why? Because Jesus had authority. **"The Father loves the Son and has given him power over everything."**

Jesus had power and authority given to him by his Father.

Why did the Pharisees plan to kill Jesus?

Luke 18:9–14; John 11:47–48

Pride is a small word that causes big problems. It was the reason the Pharisees sought to kill Jesus. "This man is doing many miracles," they said. "If we let him continue doing these things, everyone will believe in him."

Jesus told his followers a parable that teaches the lesson of **pride**. He told about a Pharisee and a tax collector who went to the temple to pray. The Pharisee thanked God that he was better than other men. But the tax collector said, "God, have mercy on me. I am a sinner!"

When you feel that you are better than other people, that's called pride. The Pharisees let pride get the best of them.

Let's not let pride get the best of us!

Why did Jesus die on a cross for me?

Matthew 20:28

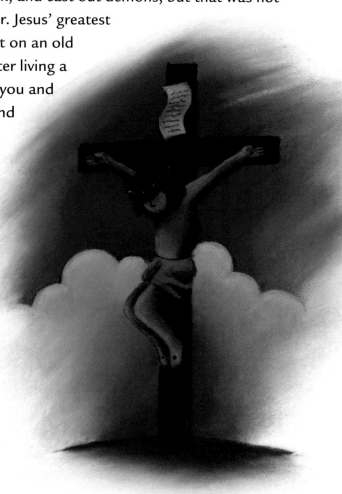

Jesus preached the most powerful sermons ever heard, but that was not enough to save us. He taught the crowds with parables, healed the sick, and cast out demons, but that was not enough to save us either. Jesus' greatest ministry was carried out on an old rugged cross. There, after living a perfect life, he died for you and me. And by his death and resurrection, Jesus gave that perfect life to you and me.

"The Son of Man came to give his life **to save** many people," Jesus said. He took our place in death. That was enough to save us!

He died to save us *from* God's wrath and to save us *to* heaven—all because he loves us.

HOW IT HAPPENED

How do we receive eternal life?

John 3:16; 5:24

Birthdays are so much fun! And the best part of a birthday is opening the gifts! A *gift* is something you receive from someone who cares about you. You don't have to pay for it. It's given freely. Someone else bought the gift and delivered it to you with a big, bright bow.

The Bible says that God has given us a gift too! It is the gift of eternal life through Jesus Christ. When Jesus died on the cross, he paid for that gift. He paid with his life because he cared so much. The gift he gave was eternal life. Because of his gift, we can live forever with him in heaven. But you have to receive it. How? It's easy . . . just pray this prayer:

> *Dear God, I believe that Jesus is your son. I know he is a gift you have given to me. Because of Jesus, I now have eternal life. By faith, I believe that Jesus has paid for my gift with his life. I receive your gift. I receive Jesus. Amen.*

We receive the gift of eternal life by accepting Jesus as our Savior.

How does Jesus want us to live?

Matthew 5:13–16; 1 Corinthians 7:31

The greatest sermon ever preached happened on a mountainside near Jerusalem. It was there that Jesus explained how he wanted us to live. "You are the salt of the earth," he said. "You are the light that gives light to the world."

What in the world did Jesus mean by that? It's hard to imagine a time when there were no refrigerators. But in Jesus' time, salt was used to keep food fresh. People would rub salt into their food to save and preserve it.

Likewise, the apostle Paul said that this world "will soon be gone," kind of like food that's not refrigerated. So we are to be like salt, "rubbing in" the gospel of Jesus to everyone we meet! We should tell people about Jesus, about how he preserves and saves!

Jesus also said we are to be a "**light** to the world." Light helps people see; it lights the path and chases away the darkness. We are to live our lives as a light to guide others to Jesus and his saving power.

How will we know when Jesus comes again?

Matthew 24:31

There are lots of instruments in an orchestra. The violin makes a sweet sound. Flutes sing the high notes, and tubas sound the low notes. But there is one instrument whose tone rises above all others—the trumpet. When the trumpet sounds, everyone can hear it. Trumpets are used to announce important events, victories, and the arrival of royalty.

Even to this day, kings and presidents are welcomed by the playing of a trumpet. So it is not surprising that the trumpet will announce the coming of the King of kings, Jesus Christ! The Bible says that **a trumpet will sound**, and every eye shall see Jesus as he breaks through the clouds. Wow!

When the trumpet sounds, the whole world will hear!

How long does salvation last?

John 3:16

Salvation is everlasting! If you had a pair of everlasting shoes, they would *never* wear out. If you had an everlasting gallon of milk, it would *never* run out. And if you had **everlasting** energy, on and on you'd go, and you would never ever stop.

On earth, we all run out of steam eventually. But God has promised everlasting life to those who accept Jesus as their Savior. That means that no matter how long you may live with Jesus in heaven, there is always one more day to live. In this world, we are born, and then someday we die. But when we are saved, John 3:16 says we receive everlasting life.

So how long does salvation last? Always one more day!

Scripture Index

Topical Index

INDEX

Names and Places